THE CODEX ALIMENTARIUS

PREFACE

The Codex Alimentarius Commission is the international body responsible for the execution of the Joint FAO/WHO Food Standards Programme. Created in 1962 by FAO and WHO the Programme is aimed at protecting the health of consumers and facilitating international trade in foods.

The Codex Alimentarius (Latin, meaning Food Law or Code) is a collection of international food standards adopted by the Commission and presented in a uniform manner. It includes standards for all the principal foods, whether processed or semi-processed or raw. Materials for further processing into foods are included to the extent necessary to achieve the purposes of the Codex Alimentarius as defined. The Codex Alimentarius includes provisions in respect of the hygienic and nutritional quality of food, including microbiological norms, provisions for food additives, pesticide residues, contaminants, labelling and presentations, and methods of analysis and sampling. It also includes provisions of an advisory nature in the form of codes of practice, guidelines and other recommended measures.

This is the second publication of the Codex Alimentarius. The first publication was in 1981. Prior to 1981 standards adopted by the Codex Alimentarius were published individually as Recommended Standards (CAC/RS series).

The Second Edition of the Codex Alimentarius is now being revised and updated to take into account decisions made by the 21st Session of the Codex Alimentarius Commission.

Joint FAO/WHO Food Standards Programme
CODEX ALIMENTARIUS COMMISSION

SUPPLEMENT 1
TO
VOLUME 5B

CODEX ALIMENTARIUS

FRESH FRUITS AND VEGETABLES

**FOOD AND AGRICULTURE ORGANIZATION
OF THE UNITED NATIONS
WORLD HEALTH ORGANIZATION**
Rome, 1996

M-83

ISBN 92-5-103848-1

TABLE OF CONTENTS

	Page
PREFACE	iii
INTRODUCTION	vii

CODEX STANDARDS

- Litchi (CODEX STAN 196-1995) 1
- Avocado (CODEX STAN 197-1995) 9

CODE OF PRACTICE

- Packaging and Transport of Fresh Fruit and Vegetables 17

INTRODUCTION

STATUTES OF THE CODEX ALIMENTARIUS COMMISSION AND IMPLEMENTATION OF THE FOOD STANDARDS PROGRAMME BY THE COMMISSION

The Codex Alimentarius Commission was established to implement the Joint FAO/WHO Food Standards Programme, the purpose of which is, as set down in the Statutes of the Commission, to protect the health of consumers and to ensure fair practices in the food trade; to promote coordination of all food standards work undertaken by international governmental and non-governmental organizations; to determine priorities and initiate and guide the preparation of draft standards through and with the aid of appropriate organizations; to finalize standards, and, after acceptance by governments, publish them in a Codex Alimentarius either as regional or world-wide standards[1].

The Statutes of the Codex Alimentarius Commission have been approved by the Governing bodies of the FAO and WHO. The Commission is a subsidiary body of these two parent Organizations. The Statutes and Rules of the Commission are to be found in the Procedural Manual of the Commission.

THE CODEX ALIMENTARIUS

PURPOSE

The Codex Alimentarius is a collection of internationally adopted food standards presented in a uniform manner. These food standards aim at protecting consumers' health and ensuring fair practices in the food trade. The Codex Alimentarius also includes provisions of an advisory nature in the form of codes of practice, guidelines and other recommended measures to assist in achieving the purposes of the Codex Alimentarius. The publication of the Codex Alimentarius is intended to guide and promote the elaboration and establishment of definitions and requirements for foods, to assist in their harmonization and, in doing so, to facilitate international trade.

SCOPE

The Codex Alimentarius includes standards for all the principal foods, whether processed, semi-processed or raw, for distribution to the consumer. Materials for further processing into foods are included to the extent necessary to achieve the purposes of the Codex Alimentarius as defined. The Codex Alimentarius includes provisions in respect of the hygienic and nutritional quality of food, including microbiological norms, provisions for food additives, pesticide residues, contaminants, labelling and presentation, and methods of analysis and sampling. It also includes provisions of an advisory nature in the form of codes of practice, guidelines and other recommended measures. Codex standards contain requirements for food aimed at ensuring for the consumer a sound, wholesome food product free from adulteration, correctly labelled and presented.

---

[1] The Codex Alimentarius Commission decided, at its 14th Session in July 1981, that its standards, which are sent to all Member States and Associate Members of FAO and/or WHO for acceptance, together with details of notifications received from governments with respect to the acceptance or otherwise of the standards and other relevant information, constitute the Codex Alimentarius.

ACCEPTANCE

The standards and maximum residue limits adopted by the Codex Alimentarius Commission are intended for formal acceptance by governments in accordance with its General Principles.

The standards and maximum limits for residues of pesticides and veterinary drugs in foods and feeds, accompanied by an appropriate communication, are sent for action to Ministries of Agriculture or Ministries of Foreign Affairs, as appropriate, of Member Nations of FAO and to Ministries of Health of Member States of WHO. The standards and maximum limits for pesticide residues and veterinary drugs, accompanied by the communication referred to, are also sent to national Codex Contact Points, FAO and WHO Regional Offices, FAO Representatives, Embassies in Rome and Permanent Missions to the UN in Geneva.

The standards and maximum limits for residues of pesticides and veterinary drugs in foods and feeds, which have taken a number of years to develop, are the product of a wide measure of international agreement and cooperation. They are compatible with the norms considered by FAO and WHO as best guaranteeing the protection of the health of consumers and the facilitation of international trade in food.

EXPLANATORY NOTES

GENERAL

The Standards included in this publication were elaborated by the Codex Committee on Tropical Fresh Fruits and Vegetables. The Joint FAO/WHO Secretariat gratefully acknowledges the important contribution of the Host Government Secretariat (Mexico) in the elaboration of these standards and in the verification of the present compiled document.

CODEX STANDARD FOR LITCHI

CODEX STAN 196 - 1995

CODEX STANDARD FOR LITCHI

CODEX STAN 196-1995

1.   DEFINITION OF PRODUCE

This standard applies to commercial litchi varieties (cultivars) grown from *Litchi chinensis* Sonn. of the *Sapindaceae* family, to be supplied fresh to the consumer after preparation and packaging. Litchis for industrial processing are excluded.[1]

2.   PROVISIONS CONCERNING QUALITY

2.1   Minimum Requirements

In all classes, subject to the special provisions for each class and to the tolerances allowed, the litchis must be:

- whole;
- sound; produce affected by rotting or deterioration such as to make it unfit for consumption is excluded;
- clean, practically free from visible foreign matter;
- practically free from pests;
- practically free from damage caused by pests;
- free from damage and abrasion;
- practically free from brown markings;
- free from abnormal external moisture, except for condensation following removal from cold storage;
- free of foreign smell and/or taste[2].

The litchis must have been carefully picked and must be sufficiently developed and mature. The development and condition of the litchis must be such that they can withstand transportation and handling and arrive at their destination in satisfactory condition.

The colouring of litchis may vary from pink to red in the case of untreated litchis; from pale yellow to pink for litchis that have been fumigated with sulphur dioxide.

---

[1]   Governments, when indicating the acceptance of the Codex Standard for Litchi, should notify the Commission which provisions of the Standard would be accepted for application at the point of import, and which provisions would be accepted for application at the point of export.

[2]   This provision allows for smell caused by a conservation agent used in compliance with corresponding regulations.

2.2   Classification

Litchis are classified into three classes:

2.2.1   Extra Class

Litchis in this class must be of superior quality. They must have the shape, development and colouring that are typical of the variety or varietal type.

They must be free of defects, with the exception of very slight superficial defects, provided that these do not affect the general appearance of the produce, the quality, the keeping quality and presentation in the package.

2.2.2   Class I

Litchis in this class must be of good quality and characteristic of the variety or varietal type. However, the following slight defects are admissible provided they do not affect the general appearance of the produce, its quality, the keeping quality or presentation in the package:

-    slight misshaping;
-    a slight colour defect;
-    slight skin defects provided these do not exceed a total area of 0.25 cm².

2.2.3   Class II

This class includes litchis which do not qualify for the higher classes but satisfy the minimum requirements listed below.

The following defects are admissible provided the litchis retain their essential characteristics as regards quality, conservation and presentation:

-    defects in shape;
-    defects in colour;
-    skin blemishes on condition that their total area does not exceed 0.5 cm².

3.   PROVISIONS CONCERNING SIZING

Size is determined by the maximum equatorial diameter.

The minimum size for Extra Class is 33 mm.

The minimum size for Classes I and II is 20 mm.

A maximum size range of 10 mm between fruit in each package is permitted.

4.   PROVISIONS CONCERNING TOLERANCES

Quality and size tolerances are allowed in each package for produce not satisfying the requirements of the class indicated.

4.1   Quality Tolerances

4.1.1   Extra Class

Five percent by number or weight of litchis not satisfying the requirements of this class, but meeting those of Class I or exceptionally, coming within the tolerances of that class.

4.1.2   Class I

Ten percent by number or weight of litchis not satisfying the requirements of this class, but meeting those of Class II or, exceptionally, coming within the tolerances of that class.

4.1.3   Class II

Ten percent by number or weight of litchis satisfying neither the requirements of this class nor the minimum requirements, with the exception of produce affected by rotting or any other deterioration rendering it unfit for consumption.

4.2   Size Tolerances

In all classes: 10% by number or weight of litchis not conforming to the minimum size, provided, however, that the diameter is not less that 15 mm in all classes, and/or the maximum size range of 10 mm.

5.   PROVISIONS CONCERNING PRESENTATION

5.1   Uniformity

The contents of each package must be uniform and only contain litchis of the same origin, variety or varietal type, quality, size and colour.

The visible part of the contents of the package must be representative of the entire contents.

5.2   Packaging

Litchis must be packed in such a way as to protect the produce properly.

The material used inside the packages must be new[3], clean and of a quality such as to avoid causing any external or internal damage to the produce. The use of materials, particularly of paper or stamps bearing trade specifications, is allowed provided the printing or labelling has been done with non-toxic ink or glue.

Litchis shall be packed in each container in compliance with the Code of Practice for the Packaging and Transport of Fresh Fruits and Vegetables. However, the presence of a limited number of fresh leaves is permitted where litchis are presented in bunches.

---

[3]   For the purpose of this standard, this includes recycled material of food-grade quality.

5.2.1   Description of Containers

The containers shall meet the quality, hygiene, ventilation and resistance characteristics to ensure suitable handling, shipping and preserving of the litchi. Packages (or lot if the produce is presented in bulk) must be free of all foreign matter and smell.

5.3   Presentation

The litchis must be presented under one of the following forms:

5.3.1   Individually

In this case the pedicel must be cut at the first knot and the maximum length of the stalk must not extend more than 2 mm beyond the top of the fruit.

Extra Class litchis must be presented individually.

5.3.2   In bunches

In this case, the bunch must include more than three attached and well-formed litchis. The branch must not exceed 15 cm in length.

6.   MARKING AND LABELLING

6.1   Containers destined for the final consumer

In addition to the requirements of the Codex General Standard for the Labelling of Prepackaged Foods (CODEX STAN 1-1985, Rev. 1-1991), the following specific provisions apply.

6.1.1   Nature of the produce

If the produce is not visible, each package must bear a label with the name of the produce and, optionally, that of the variety or varietal type.

6.2   Non-Retail Containers

Each package must bear the following particulars, in letters grouped on the same side, legibly and indelibly marked and visible from the outside or on accompanying documents.[4]

For products transported in bulk these particulars must appear on a document accompanying the goods.

6.2.1   Identification

Exporter, packer and/or dispatcher.

---

[4]   When accepting this Codex Standard, governments should notify the Commission which of these provisions applies.

6.2.2   Nature of the Produce

Name of produce if the contents are not visible from the outside; name of variety or commercial type (if applicable). "Bunch" specification, when applicable.

6.2.3   Origin of Produce

Country of origin and optionally, district where grown or national, regional or local place name.

6.2.4   Commercial Identification

- Class;
- Net weight (optional).

6.2.5   Official Inspection Mark (optional)

7.   **CONTAMINANTS**

7.1   **Heavy Metals**

Litchi shall be free from heavy metals in amounts which may represent a hazard to human health.

7.2   **Pesticide Residues**

Litchi shall comply with those maximum residue limits established by the Codex Alimentarius Commission for this Commodity.

8.   **HYGIENE**

8.1   It is recommended that the produce covered by the provisions of this standard be prepared and handled in accordance with the appropriate sections of the Recommended International Code of Practice - General Principles of Food Hygiene (CAC/RCP 1-1969, Rev. 2-1985), and other Codes of Practice recommended by the Codex Alimentarius Commission which are relevant to this produce.

8.2   To the extent possible in good packaging and handling practice, the produce shall be free from objectionable matter.

8.3   When tested by appropriate methods of sampling and examination, the produce:

- shall be free from microorganisms in amounts which may represent a hazard to health;

- shall be free from parasites which may represent a hazard to health; and

- shall not contain any substance originating from microorganisms in amounts which may represent a hazard to health.

CODEX STANDARD FOR AVOCADO

CODEX STAN 197 - 1995

CODEX STANDARD FOR AVOCADO

CODEX STAN 197-1995

1.   DEFINITION OF PRODUCE

This standard applies to avocados of varieties (cultivars) grown from *Persea americana* Mill. (Syn. *Persea gratissima* Gaertn) of the *Lauraceae* family, to be supplied fresh to the consumer, parthenocarpic fruit and avocados for industrial processing being excluded.[1]

2.   PROVISIONS CONCERNING QUALITY

2.1   Minimum requirements

In all classes, subject to the special provisions for each class and the tolerances allowed, the avocados must be:

- whole;
- sound; produce affected by rotting or deterioration such as to make it unfit for consumption is excluded;
- clean, practically free of any visible foreign matter;
- practically free from pests;
- practically free from damage caused by pests;
- free of damage caused by low temperature;
- having a stalk not more than 10 mm in length which must be cut off cleanly. However, its absence is not considered a defect providing that the place of the stalk attachment is dry and whole;
- free of abnormal external moisture, except for condensation following removal from cold storage;
- free of any foreign smell and/or taste.

Avocados must be carefully picked. Their development should have reached a physiological stage which will ensure a continuation of the maturation process to completion. The mature fruit should be free from bitterness.

The development and condition of the avocados must be such as to enable them to withstand transport and handling, and to arrive in satisfactory condition at the place of destination.

---

[1]   Governments, when indicating the acceptance of the Codex standard for avocado, should notify the Commission which provisions of the standard would be accepted for application at the point of import, and which provisions would be accepted for application at the point of export.

2.2 Classification

Avocados are classified into three classes defined below:

2.2.1 "Extra" Class

Avocados in this class must be of superior quality. In shape and colouring they must be characteristic of the variety.

They must be free from defects, with the exception of very slight superficial defects of the skin provided that these do not affect the general appearance of the produce, the quality, the keeping quality and presentation in the package. If present, the stalk must be intact.

2.2.2 Class I

Avocados in this class must be of good quality and show the typical colour and shape of the variety. The following slight defects, however, may be allowed provided that these do not affect the general appearance of the produce, the quality, the keeping quality and presentation in the package.

- slight defects of shape and colour;
- slight skin defects (corkiness, healed lenticels) and sunburn; the maximum total area should not exceed 4 cm^2.

In no case may the defects affect the fruit flesh.

The stalk, if present, may be slightly damaged.

2.2.3 Class II

This class includes avocados which do not qualify for inclusion in the higher classes but satisfy the minimum requirements specified above.

The following defects may be allowed provided that the avocados retain their essential characteristics as regards the quality, the keeping quality and presentation:

- defects in shape and colouring;
- skin defects (corkiness, healed lenticels) and sunburn; maximum total area should not exceed 6 cm^2.

In no case may the defects affect the fruit flesh.

The stalk, if present, may be damaged.

3.   **PROVISIONS CONCERNING SIZING**

Size is determined by the weight of the fruit; the size scale is as follows[2]:

Weight scale (grammes)	Code size
> 1220	2
781 to 1 220	4
576 to 780	6
461 to 575	8
366 to 460	10
306 to 365	12
266 to 305	14
236 to 265	16
211 to 235	18
191 to 210	20
171 to 190	22
156 to 170	24
146 to 155	26
136 to 145	28
125 to 135	30

The minimum weight of avocados must not be less than 125 g.

4.   **PROVISIONS CONCERNING TOLERANCES**

Tolerances in respect of quality and size shall be allowed in each package for produce not satisfying the requirements for the class indicated.

4.1   **Quality tolerances**

4.1.1   "Extra" Class

5 per cent by number or weight of avocados not satisfying the requirements of the class but meeting those of Class I or, exceptionally, coming within the tolerances of that class.

4.1.2   Class I

10 per cent by number or weight of avocados not satisfying the requirements of the class but meeting those of Class II or, exceptionally, coming within the tolerances of that class.

---

[2]   Nevertheless, no account should be taken for a given fruit of a deviation of more or less than 2 per cent with regard to the code number indicated.

4.1.3 Class II

10 per cent by number or weight of avocados not meeting the requirements of the class nor the minimum requirements, with the exception of fruit affected by rotting, marked bruising or any other deterioration rendering it unfit for consumption.

4.2 Size tolerances

For all classes: 10 per cent, by number or weight of avocados corresponding to the size immediately above or below those indicated in Section 3.

5. PROVISIONS CONCERNING PRESENTATION

5.1 Uniformity

The contents of each package must be uniform and contain only avocados of the same origin, variety, quality and size. The visible part of the contents of the package must be representative of the entire contents.

5.2 Packaging

Avocados must be packed in such a way so as to protect the produce properly.

The materials used inside the package must be new[3], clean and of a quality such as to avoid causing any external or internal damage to the fruit. The use of materials, particularly of paper or stamps bearing trade specifications, is allowed provided that the printing or labelling has been done with a non-toxic ink or glue.

Avocados shall be packed in each container in compliance with the Code of Practice for the Packaging and Transport of Fresh Fruits and Vegetables.

5.2.1 Description of Containers

The containers shall meet the quality, hygiene, ventilation and resistance characteristics to ensure suitable handling, shipping and preserving of the avocado. Packages must be free of all foreign matter and smell.

6. MARKING OR LABELLING

6.1 Containers destined for the final consumer

In addition to the requirements of the Codex General Standard for the Labelling of Prepacked Foods (CODEX STAN 1-1985, Rev. 1-1991) the following specific provisions apply:

---

[3] For the purpose of this standard, this includes recycled material of food-grade quality.

6.1.1   Nature of the Produce

If the product is not visible, each package shall be labelled as to the name of the food and may be labelled as to the name of the variety.

6.2   Non Retail Containers

Each package must bear the following particulars, in letters grouped on the same side, legibly and indelibly marked and visible from the outside, or in the documents accompanying the shipment.[4]

For products transported in bulk these particulars must appear on a document accompanying the goods.

6.2.1   Identification

Exporter, Packer and/or dispatcher.

6.2.2   Nature of the produce

Name of produce if the contents are not visible from the outside.   Name of variety or commercial type (if applicable).

6.2.3   Origin of produce

Country of origin and, optionally, district where grown, or national, regional or local place name.

6.2.4   Commercial Identification

- Class;
- Size expressed in minimum and maximum weight;
- Code number of the size scale and number of fruits when it is different from reference number;
- Net weight (optional).

6.2.5   Official Inspection Mark (optional)

7.   CONTAMINANTS

7.1   Heavy Metals

Avocado shall be free from heavy metals in amounts which may represent a hazard to human health.

---

[4]   Governments, when indicating their acceptance of this Codex Standard, should notify the Commission as to which provisions of this section apply.

7.2   **Pesticide Residues**

Avocado shall comply with those maximum residue limits established by the Codex Alimentarius Commission for this Commodity.

8.   **HYGIENE**

8.1   It is recommended that the produce covered by the provisions of this standard be prepared and handled in accordance with the appropriate sections of the Recommended International Code of Practice - General Principles of Food Hygiene (CAC/RCP 1-1969, Rev. 2-1985), and other Codes of Practice recommended by the Codex Alimentarius Commission which are relevant to this produce.

8.2   To the extent possible in good packaging and handling practice, the produce shall be free from objectionable matter.

8.3   When tested by appropriate methods of sampling and examination, the produce:

- shall be free from microorganisms in amounts which may represent a hazard to health;

- shall be free from parasites which may represent a hazard to health; and

- shall not contain any substance originating from microorganisms in amounts which may represent a hazard to health.

RECOMMENDED INTERNATIONAL CODE OF PRACTICE FOR PACKAGING AND TRANSPORT OF FRESH FRUIT AND VEGETABLES

CAC/RCP 44 - 1995

RECOMMENDED INTERNATIONAL CODE OF PRACTICE FOR PACKAGING AND TRANSPORT OF TROPICAL FRESH FRUIT AND VEGETABLES

CAC/RCP 44 - 1995

- *SECTION I* -

SCOPE

1.1   This code recommends proper packaging and transport of fresh fruit and vegetables in order to maintain produce quality during transportation and marketing.

- *SECTION II* -

DESIGN, CONDITION AND LOADING METHOD OF TRANSPORT EQUIPMENT

2.1   **Mode of transportation and type of equipment**

Factors include:

- destination;
- value of the produce;
- degree of produce perishability;
- amount of produce to be transported;
- recommended storage temperature and relative humidity;
- outside temperature conditions at origin and destination points;
- time in transit to reach destination by air, land, or ocean transport;
- freight rates negotiated with the carriers;
- quality of transportation service.

2.2   **Reliability and quality of transportation service provided by different carriers must be carefully considered along with the rates charged.** Services and schedules are established or modified weekly. Sometimes service is abruptly withdrawn. Shippers should contact air and ocean port authorities at their origin and destination locations to receive the most current information on available services. Local trade publications also are excellent sources of information, as many carriers and their agents advertise their schedules and destinations.

2.3   **When available refrigerated trailers and van containers are recommended for most high volume produce with transit and storage lives of a week or more.** After transit, there must be enough remaining produce life for marketing. Carriers utilizing trailers and containers can offer a door-to-door service. This reduces handling, exposure, damage, and theft of the produce.

2.4   **Air cargo containers also can be used to provide a door-to-door service.** Produce transported by air is generally high-value and highly perishable. Freight costs are higher by air. Transit times, however, are in terms of hours instead of days.

2.5   **Many produce is shipped in unrefrigerated air containers or on air cargo pallets**. This requires close coordination at the origin and destination airports to protect the produce when flights are delayed. Temperature-controlled storage facilities at airports are needed to ensure produce quality. Refrigerated air containers are available and should be used when possible. Use of insulated thermal blankets is an option.

2.6   **Produce which can be shipped in refrigerated trailers and van containers are sometimes shipped by air to take advantage of brief market opportunities, such as the beginning of a season when prices are high and supply is limited.** A robust and accurate system for monitoring or displaying temperature and relative humidity during transport in integral containers needs to be considered.

2.7   **Long distance transportation through tropical and frigid climates requires rugged well-designed equipment to withstand the transit environment and protect the produce.** Desirable features in refrigerated trailers up to 14.6 m (48 ft) long and van containers up to 12 m (40 ft) long include for example:

- 42,000 kJ/h (40,000 BTU/h) refrigeration capacity at 38°C (100°F) ambient, 2°C (36°F) return air temperature.

- a continuously operating high capacity evaporator blower for more even produce temperatures and higher relative humidities;

- a solid return air bulkhead at the front of the trailer to ensure air circulation throughout the load;

- vertical ribs on the rear door to assist in air circulation;

- adequate insulation and provisions for heating, when used in regions where weather conditions so demand due to the nature of the produce;

- deep floor grooves or channels, from 50 to 75 mm (2 to 3 mm) in depth to provide an adequate cross-sectional area for air circulation under loads placed directly on the floor;

- supply-air temperature sensing of the operation of the refrigeration unit to reduce produce chilling and freezing injury;

- provisions for ventilation to prevent ethylene or carbon dioxide buildup;

- air-ride suspension to reduce the amount of shock and vibration transferred to the shipping containers and the produce inside.

- modern containers in which cold air leaves the front part of the container, but the air flow circulates from below (close to the floor) toward the back, then rising to the upper part of the container.

2.8   **Most carriers check their transport equipment before presenting it to the shipper for loading**. The condition of the equipment is critical to maintaining the quality of the produce. Therefore, the shipper also should check the equipment to ensure it is in good working order and meets the needs of the produce. Carriers provide guidance on checking and operating the refrigeration systems.

2.9   All transportation equipment should be checked for:

-   cleanliness--the load compartment should be regularly cleaned for example by steam cleaning;

-   damage to walls, floors, doors, ceilings should be in good condition;

-   temperature control--refrigerated units should be recently calibrated and supply continuous air circulation for uniform produce temperatures.

2.10   Shippers should insist on clean equipment. A load of produce can be ruined by:

-   smell from previous deliveries or incompatible loads;
-   toxic chemical residues;
-   insects nesting in the equipment;
-   decaying remains of agricultural produce;
-   debris blocking drain openings or air circulation channels along the floor.

2.11   Shippers should insist on well maintained equipment and check for the following:

-   damage to walls, ceilings, or floors which can let in the outside heat, cold, moisture, dirt, and insects;

-   operation and condition of doors, ventilation openings, and seals;

-   provisions for load locking and bracing.

2.12   For refrigerated trailers and van containers, the following additional checks are important:

-   with the doors closed, have someone inside the cargo area check for light--door gaskets must seal. A smoke generator also can be used to detect leaks;

-   the refrigeration unit should cycle from high to low speed when the desired temperature is reached and then back to high speed;

-   determine the location of the sensing element which controls the discharge air temperature. If it measures return air temperature, the thermostat may have to be set-higher to avoid chilling injury or freezing injury of the produce;

-   a solid return air bulkhead should be installed at the front of the trailer;

-   a heating device should be available for transportation in areas with extreme cold weather;

-   equipment with a top air delivery system should have a fabric air chute or metal ceiling duct in good condition.

2.13   **Produce requiring refrigeration should be thoroughly precooled, if necessary, prior to loading into transportation equipment**. Produce temperatures should be taken with an appropriate thermometer and recorded on the bill of lading for future reference. The load compartment in the equipment also should be precooled to the recommended transport or storage temperature for the produce. It is advisable that the loading area should be enclosed and if available, the loading dock doorway area should be equipped with doorway air seals.

2.14   **Proper loading practices are critical to maintaining temperature and relative humidity, protecting the produce from impact and vibration forces in transit, and preventing insects from entering the load.** Special care must be taken when shipping mixed loads. The produce must be compatible.

2.15   Basic loading methods include:

- bulk loading, by machine or hand, of unpackaged commodities;

- hand loading individual shipping containers, with or without pallets;

- unit loading of palletized or slipsheet loads of containers with pallet jacks or forklifts.

2.16   **Inadequate provisions for air circulation will ruin a load, even in well designed transportation equipment.** When possible, shipping containers should be kept off shallow floors and away from flat sidewalls by using pallets, racks, and dunnage. Adequate head space between the upper row of cartons and the top of the container should be allowed; this may be done by taping or gluing the upper row of cartons or by using appropriately designed packages for this purpose. Room for air circulation must be provided under, around and through the load to protect the produce from:

- heat gain from the outside air during hot weather;
- heat generated by the produce through respiration;
- accumulation of ethylene from ripening of the produce;
- heat loss to the outside air during extreme cold weather;
- chilling injury or freezing injury during operation of the refrigeration unit.

2.17   **Shippers using refrigerated transport equipment should follow the carrier's recommendations on loading of the equipment's load compartment to avoid chilling injury or freezing injury to the produce.** Discharge air may be colder than the set-point temperature if the refrigeration system operates on return air temperature sensing.

2.18   Loads should be secured with one or more of the following materials to prevent the effects of vibrations and impact damage in transport and handling:

- aluminum or wood load locks;
- paperboard or fibreboard honeycomb fillers;
- wood blocking and nailing strips;
- inflatable kraft paper air bags;
- cargo nets and straps;
- wood load gates constructed of 25 mm x 100 mm (1 x 4 in) material.

2.19 **If available all loads should have a small air temperature recorder placed between packages in the area where the warmest temperatures occur.** Recorder companies recommend placement on top of the load, near a side wall, one-third of the way in from the rear doors, away from any direct discharge of refrigerated air. Rail cars should have two or three recorders. In loads with top-ice or humidity above 95 percent, the recorders should be waterproof or enclosed in a plastic bag.

2.19.1 Shippers and receivers must follow the temperature recorder companies instructions on documenting the load, starting the recorder, reading the results, and returning it for calibration and certification if necessary. These steps are essential for settling claims over temperature management during transportation.

2.20 **Similar sized shipping containers should be loaded together in mixed loads for increased stability.** Heavier shipping containers of produce should be loaded first, distributed evenly across the floor of the trailer or container. Lighter shipping containers can then be placed against or on top of the heavier produce. Load lock and secure stacks of different sized shipping containers. To facilitate inspection of mixed loads at ports of entry, a representative sample of each commodity should be available near the door. This can minimize the unloading of cargo for examination.

2.21 **Never load fruit, vegetables, or other food products with cargoes that provide any risk of contamination through transfer of odour or toxic chemical residues.** The longer the transit time, the higher the risks in transporting mixed loads of agricultural produce. Therefore it is essential that guidelines be followed as much as possible to maintain quality in distant markets.

2.22 **Modified atmospheres of reduced oxygen and elevated carbon dioxide and nitrogen are provided to trailers and containers after loading is completed.** The trailers and containers must be equipped with channels at the doorway for a plastic film curtain and gas ports for the application of the treatment.

2.23 **The refrigeration unit, walls, ceiling, floor, and doors must adequately seal the inside of the cargo area from outside air.** Otherwise the modified atmosphere will quickly dissipate. Warning labels must be applied to the equipment to warn that the atmosphere is not life supporting and that the cargo area must be properly ventilated before personnel enter to unload the cargo.

- SECTION III -

PACKAGING TO MAINTAIN PRODUCE QUALITY DURING TRANSPORTATION AND MARKETING

3.1 Packaging must withstand:

- rough handling during loading and unloading;
- compression from the overhead weight of other containers;
- impact and vibration during transportation;
- high humidity during precooling, transit, and storage.

3.2 **Packaging materials are chosen on the basis of needs of the produce, packing method, precooling method, strength, cost, availability, buyer specifications, and freight rates.** Importers, buyers, and packaging manufacturers provide valuable recommendations. Materials used include:

- paperboard or fibreboard bins, boxes (glued, stapled, interlocking), lugs, trays, flats, dividers or partitions, and slipsheets;

- wood bins, crates (wirebound, nailed), baskets, trays, lugs, pallets;

- paper bags, sleeves, wraps, liners, pads, excelsior, and labels;

- plastic bins, boxes, trays, bags (mesh, solid), containers, sleeves, film wraps, liners, dividers, and slipsheets;

- foam boxes, trays, lugs, sleeves, liners, dividers, and pads.

3.3   **Bins, boxes, crates, trays, lugs, baskets, and bags are considered shipping containers**. Baskets, however, are difficult to handle in mixed loads of rectangular boxes. Bags provide limited produce protection. The fibreboard type box is a widely used container. Styles include for example:

- one-piece slotted box with glued, stapled, or self-locking flaps;

- two-piece half slotted box with a cover;

- two-piece half slotted box with a full telescoping cover, providing strong walls and corners;

- three-piece Bliss-style box featuring stapled or glued ends providing strong corners;

- one-piece box with full telescoping cover;

- two-piece, die-cut style box with full telescoping cover;

- one-piece box with wire or fibreboard tabs or hardboard end inserts and plastic end caps, providing stacking strength and alignment.

3.3.1   **Fibreboard boxes for produce which are packed wet or with ice must be wax-impregnated or coated with water resistant material**. The compression strength of untreated fibreboard can be reduced more than one half in conditions of 90 percent relative humidity. In addition to maintaining box strength, wax helps to reduce the loss of moisture from the produce to the fibreboard. All glued boxes should be made with a water resistant adhesive.

3.3.2   The majority of fibreboard boxes and wood crates are designed to be stacked top to bottom. Compression strength and produce protection are sacrificed when boxes or crates are stacked on their ends or sides. Misaligned boxes can lose up to 50 percent of their top to bottom compression strength.

3.4   **Various materials are added to shipping containers to provide additional strength and produce protection**. Dividers or partitions and double or triple thickness sides and ends in fibreboard boxes provide additional compression strength and reduce produce damage.

3.4.1   Pads, wraps, and sleeves and excelsior also reduce bruising. Pads also are used to provide moisture as with asparagus; provide chemical treatment to reduce decay as with sulphur dioxide pads for grapes; and absorb ethylene as with potassium permanganate pads in boxes of bananas and flowers.

3.4.2   Plastic film liners or bags are used to retain moisture. Perforated plastic is used for most produce to allow exchange of gases and avoid excessive humidity. Solid plastic is used to seal the produce and provide for modified atmosphere by reducing the amount of oxygen available for respiration and ripening. For example, this is done for bananas, strawberries, tomatoes and citrus fruits.

3.5   Packing methods include:

- field packing - produce is placed in fibreboard boxes, plastic crates or wood crates during harvesting. Some produce is wrapped. The filled containers are then taken to a precooling facility to have the field heat removed where possible;

- shed packing - produce is processed or packed indoors or under cover at a central location. The produce is brought from the field to the packing shed in bulk in field crates, bins, or trucks. If available, the produce should be precooled either before or after they are placed in shipping containers according to the nature of the produce;

- repacking - produce is taken out of one container, regraded, and placed in another. This is often done to make smaller containers for the retailer or consumer packages.

3.5.1   Types of packs include:

- volume fill - produce is placed by hand or machine into the container until the desired capacity, weight, or count is reached;

- tray or cell pack - produce is placed in moulded trays or cells which provide separation and reduced bruising;

- place pack - produce is carefully placed in the container. This provides reduced bruising and a pleasing appearance;

- consumer pack or prepack - relatively small amounts of produce are packaged, weighted, and labelled for retail sale;

- film or shrink wrap - each fruit or vegetable is individually wrapped and sealed in film to reduce moisture loss and decay. The film may be treated with authorized fungicides or other chemicals;

- modified atmosphere - individual consumer packs, shipping containers, or pallet loads of containers are sealed with plastic film or bags. The oxygen level is reduced and the carbon dioxide level is increased. This reduces produce respiration and slows the ripening process.

3.6   **Shipping containers must be sized and filled correctly**. Containers which are very wide and weight more than 23 kg (50 lb), for example, encourage rougher handling, produce damage, and container failure. Overfilling causes produce bruising and excessive bulging of the sides of the container, which leads to decreased compression strength and container failure. Under-filling also causes produce damage. The produce is bruised as it moves around inside the shipping container during transport and handling.

Packaging and Transport of   - 26 -
Fresh Fruit and Vegetables   Codex Alimentarius
CAC/RCP 44-1995   *Volume 5B - Sup. 1 - 1995*

3.6.1   Due to large number of different container sizes in use, box standards are desirable.

Standardized containers:

- utilize, with other containers, the maximum surface of the pallet with no overhang and little underhang;

- provide unit loads and stable mixed pallet loads;

- reduce transportation and marketing costs.

3.7   **A large number of shippers have switched from handling individual shipping containers to unit loads on pallets.** Most distribution centres are set up to store palletized loads in three tier racks.

3.7.1   Unit loads provide for:

- reduced handling of individual shipping containers;
- less damage to the containers and the produce inside;
- faster loading and unloading of transportation equipment;
- more efficient distribution centre operations.

3.7.2   Unit loads may include, for example, some of the following features:

- standard wood pallets or slipsheets such as; 1200 x 1000 mm (48 x 40in), 800 x 1000 mm, 800 x 1200 mm, 1000 x 1200 mm;

- fibreboard, plastic or wire vertical interlocking tabs between boxes;

- boxes with holes for air circulation, which align when the boxes are stacked squarely on top of one another, corner to corner;

- glue between boxes to resist horizontal slipping;

- plastic netting around the pallet load of boxes;

- fibreboard, plastic, or metal cornerboards;

- plastic or metal strapping around the cornerboards and boxes.

3.8   **Wood pallets must be strong enough to allow storage under load.** Provisions for forklift and pallet jack handling are necessary. The design of the bottom of the pallet should not block air circulation.

3.8.1   Pallets must have an adequate number of top deck boards to support fibreboard boxes. Otherwise the boxes may collapse between deck boards from the overhead weight of the other containers, crush the produce, and cause the entire load to lean or fall off the pallet. A sheet of fibreboard with holes for air circulation can be used to distribute air across the pallet.

3.8.2   Boxes must not overhang the edges of the pallets. Overhang can reduce the strength of fibreboard boxes by one-third. This condition also can lead to collapse of the entire load, crushing of the produce, and make loading, unloading, and storage in racks difficult. On the other hand, boxes which utilize less than 90 percent of the pallet surface and do not align with the pallet edge can shift in transit.

3.8.3   Pallet loads of shipping containers which are not strapped or netted should have at least the top three layers of containers cross-stacked to provide stability. Some shippers use film wrap, tape, or glue on the top layers in addition to cross-stacking. The containers must be strong enough to be cross-stacked without collapsing. Film wrap should not be used on shipping containers of produce that need ventilation.

3.9   **Slipsheets are used by some shippers because they cost less than pallets**. They also eliminate the cost of transporting and returning pallets. A special forklift is needed to transfer slipsheet loads to and from the pallets at the shipper's and receiver's distribution centre. If a receiver does not have the proper handling equipment, the packages are unloaded by hand onto pallets for placement in storage. Shipping containers on slipsheets are cross-stacked, film wrapped, or otherwise unitized with cornerboards and strapping.

3.9.1   Slipsheets made of fibreboard or plastic must be strong enough to be clamped and pulled onto the forklift tines or plate for lifting while fully loaded. Fibreboard slipsheets should be wax impregnated when used in wet conditions. Slipsheets used in transportation equipment should have holes for air circulation under the load. The use of slipsheets in refrigerated transportation equipment with shallow floor channels is not recommended due to the need for adequate air circulation under the load.

- SECTION IV -

PRECOOLING PRACTICES

4.1   If available, the removal of field heat by the process of precooling to a recommended storage temperature and relative humidity is suggested to maintain the quality of fruits, and vegetables. The quality of most produce will rapidly deteriorate if field heat is not removed before loading into transportation equipment.

4.2   Refrigerated transportation equipment is designed to maintain temperature and should not be used to remove field heat from produce packed in shipping containers. The refrigeration units also are not capable of raising or controlling the relative humidity.

4.3   Precooling extends produce life by reducing:

- field heat;
- the rate of respiration and heat generated by the produce;
- the rate of ripening;
- the loss of moisture (shrivelling and wilting);
- the production of ethylene (ripening gas generated by the produce);
- the spread of decay.

4.4   The success of precooling is dependent on:

- time between harvest and precooling;
- type of shipping container if produce is packed beforehand;
- initial produce temperature;
- velocity or amount of cold air, water, or ice provided;
- final produce temperature;
- sanitation of the precooling air or water to reduce decay organisms.
- maintenance of the recommended temperature after precooling.

4.5   Precooling, where it is used, should occur as soon as possible after harvest. For most produce, harvesting should be done in early morning hours to minimize field heat and the refrigeration load on precooling equipment. Harvested produce should be protected from the sun with covering until they are placed in the precooling facility.

4.6   Many products are field or shed packed and then precooled. Wirebound wood or nailed crates or wax impregnated fibreboard boxes are used for packed produce that are precooled with water or ice after packing. Precooling of produce packed in shipping containers and stacked in unitized pallet loads is especially important as air circulation around and through the packaging may be limited during transportation and storage.

4.7   The choice of precooling method depends on the nature, value, and quality of the produce as well as the cost of labour, equipment, and materials. Precooling methods include:

- room cooling--stacking containers of produce in a refrigerated room. Some produce is misted or sprayed with water during room cooling;

- forced air cooling or wet pressure cooling-drawing air through stacks of containers of produce in a refrigerated room. For some produce, water is added to the air;

- hydrocooling--flushing produce in bulk tanks, bins, or shipping containers with a large quantity of ice water;

- vacuum cooling--removing heat from produce packed in shipping containers by drawing a vacuum in a chamber;

- hydrovacuum cooling--adding moisture to produce packed in shipping containers before or during the vacuum process, to speed the removal of heat;

- package-icing--injecting slush or crushed ice into each shipping container of produce. Some operations use bulk containers.

4.8   Since most produce is sensitive to chilling injury, care must be taken not to precool or store the produce below the recommended temperature. Often the visible effects of chilling injury are delayed until the produce is offered for retail sale. These effects include failure to ripen properly, pitting, decay, watery breakdown, and discoloration in fruits and vegetables.

4.9   All produce is sensitive to decay. Precooling equipment and water should be sanitized continuously, for example, with a hypochlorite solution to eliminate decay producing organisms. Care also must be taken not to allow produce to warm up after precooling. Condensation on cool produce surfaces at higher air temperatures also spreads decay.

4.10   The method of transportation, condition of the transport equipment, loading method, and transit and storage practices affect the success of precooling. If the recommended temperature and relative humidity are not maintained after precooling, produce quality will deteriorate.